ACKNOWLEDG[E]

Grateful thanks to:- Thora Lindenmayer for the use of the recipes included.
My family, Roger and Sarah, for their support, as well as other family members and friends
Roger Mapes for the illustrations
The Davy and Whitehand families and friends.

Cover Design: Roger Mapes

First Published 2008 by **K.T.Publications,** 52 London Road, Kessingland,
Lowestoft, Suffolk, NR33 7PW **TEL: 01502 740 539**

All rights reserved.
No part of this publication may be copied, reproduced, stored in a retrieval
system or transmitted in any form or by any means, electrical, mechanical,
photocopy, recorded or otherwise without the prior permission of the publisher.

I.S.B.N. 0 9539046-7-9

© 2008 Catherine Mapes

These stories are dedicated to the memory of my Father.

Catherine has managed to do something very important to bring together a wonderful collection of Norfolk cameos which are yet another important contribution to literary culture and plays its part in preserving it.
Martin Kirby – Eastern Daily Press Columnist.

Anyone with an ear for Norfolk humour in a genuine Norfolk accent might very well enjoy this original collection of aptly-titled stories from the pen of Catherine Mapes.   *Russell Bower – Suffolk Author*

They'll add to the jollity of Norfolk 'Boy John'-ish celebrations of our past, I am sure.   *John Loveday*

Preface

Three Norfolk Lads with the best of intentions get themselves into many a scrape.

George tells a humorous tale of growing up in a local village in the early twentieth century with his two pals, *Charlie* the ringleader with brainwaves and the slow and steady *Bert*.

This is fiction with an authentic background, giving the reader the chance to go back to an age of innocence, jolly hard work and some rare good times.

"We laughed till we cried," George confides recalling the sight of Charlie's 'bare faced cheek' at Great Yarmouth when the moth holes turned up in his swimming costume!

Many hilarious situations are portrayed of life as many remember it. The illustrations by Roger Mapes capture the humorous mood.

"Here's one I trod in earlier"

We Three

Thass a rummon how I can remember clearly what happened donkeys years ago, yet I can't remember what I had for dinner yesterday.

Hold you hard, I say to myself, stories of what I had for dinner wouldn't be that interesting. It could be boring old custard over and over again. Howsomever, I've got a number of tales up my sleeve about what us lads got up to in the olden days.

My name's George and I lived a fairly normal but uninteresting existence for at least the first twelve years of my life. Milly and Lily, my big sisters were in service in Norwich. On the rare occasions they did come home they'd be busy showing father and mother their latest new hats or some feminine garment. Father weren't that excited either. Then there was young Gerald, still a baby and all wet and windy. I couldn't take him for a game of football.

We lived in a thatched cottage by the side of the common at Great Troshenham. Father used to paint the outside of the cottage so that it looked very smart like on them chocolate boxes. Mother used to hand sew pretty curtains. They were both very hard working.

Much further up the common lived Bert. I can picture him now with his straight brown hair and round face which always had a very worried expression as though he had a lot of responsibility. I'd see him walking past slowly with a row of little'uns behind him like a mother duck out with her ducklings.

Life changed for Bert and myself when a new family arrived. They came to live about midway between the two of us. Charlie was to be our leader. He had older brothers who were away seeking their fortune and a sister at the toddler stage. All three of us needed companions of our own age even though we came from quite big families.

One Saturday morning there was a loud knock at the door. "You answer it George, my hands are all flour," whispered mother, who was trained as a pastry cook and made really good pies and tarts.

I opened the door and there stood a tall, thin boy with fair hair and a wide grin.

"I'm Charlie, just moved in," he say.

"Can you come out this morning? Next door's cow is missing and I thought we could chase it up."

"Don't you chase it," laughed mother. Turning to me, she suggested, "Why don't you two ask Bert to go along as well. He's not been too well I've heard. The fresh air will do him good."

I wouldn't have gone round to Bert's on my own. We hadn't had much to do with each other, yet we had quite a lot in common. I suppose I was a bit like him to look at, same colour hair but mine had a quiff that wouldn't stay flat. We were both very busy on Sunday but Bert belonged to the Methodist Church in the next village and I was in the choir at the church further up the common.

Well, in next to no time Charlie had led me up to Bert's house, got permission from Bert's mother to bring back the cow and the three of us were away. It felt really good I can tell you. Us lads talked and talked and you would never believe that Charlie was a newcomer. We found later that he always fitted in wherever he went and he had moved around a lot.

I couldn't believe that he knew Billy and Betty who had the cottage farm. I used to see the hens pecking away as I went past and had seen the cow wandering about the common. The gates usually stopped her going far. "To tell you the truth, I've got a bit of a conscience about this old cow," muttered

Charlie. "I couldn't exactly be sure I shut the gate as I came back from exploring Bluebell Lane early this morning. You see I couldn't sleep and I thought to myself 'It's no good saying I'm in the country if I'm in bed'. So up I got and out I went. Then I remembered that Mother had said it would be a really lovely idea if I made her and father an early morning cup of tea after all the hard work of removing ourselves and the furniture yesterday. So I rushed back."

Charlie had a heart of gold, I might add.

"Don't you worry," I say, "We'll soon find that old cow. That aint as though we're after a racehorse."

Over the common we went, passing a deep hole where sand and gravel had been dug out and was now grassed over, through the gate and up the lane. We passed one house where a little yappy dog was barking at the gate and after a few minutes we arrived at the woods where the bluebells were in bloom. There through a wide gap in the hedge was the cow standing in the midst of the bluebells staring at us with huge eyes.

"Let's call her Bluebell," giggled Charlie. Bert started to walk up to her and she took a step towards him and he backed off in alarm.

Charlie say, "I'll get behind her and you two go a bit past the gap. Then if I shoo her out and you come back she'll have to go down the hill again."

This all worked out well. Us lads felt whully pleased as we came down the hill following Bluebell. Unfortunately I wasn't looking where I was walking. That old cow must have had a stop on the way up. I had missed the cow pat one way but now I stood right in it! The others had a laugh and I soon joined them.

"Pooh," they say. "You smell of the farmyard!"

Of course we hadn't thought to close the gate to the common as we played 'Follow the Cow' but that made it easier to get her through and close it after her.

Billy and Betty were very thankful that we had found Bluebell. They were out looking for her on the common, calling Daisy, her real name. Of course we never let on about how the gate had come to be left open in the first place.

That was the start of. some rare good times.

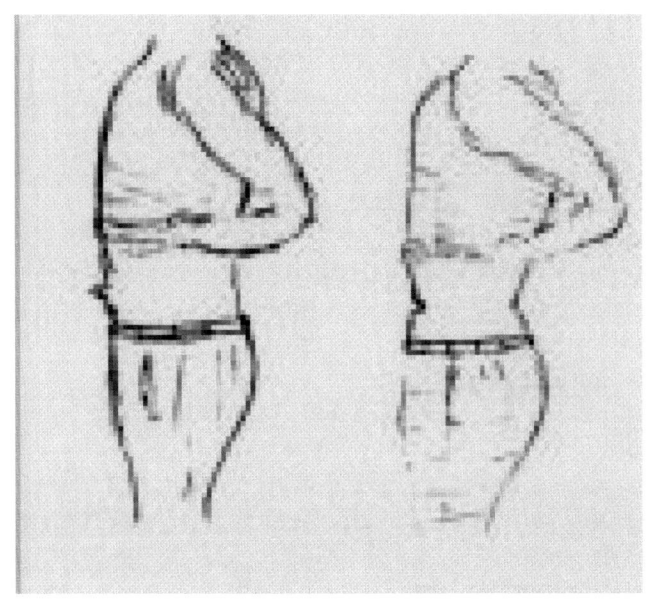

"Bert's belly button went out where Charlie's and George's went in"

Bert's Little Problem

Bert had a problem. It were of a rather delicate nature. He said it were a very private part of his body.

"Do you mean thass below your waist?" We asked him.

He thought hard and then said, "No, not really."

"If that eernt below your waist, that eernt private," grinned Charlie. "Come on. Let's have a look!"

We were in the front room of Charlie's house at the time. After a bit of deliberating we decided to go down the garden.

We sat in the long grass behind the privy eying Bert expectantly - No inside toilets in those days - There was a bit of a whiff but we were on our own.

"Well, out with it," I said, like I usually did when he had a furrowed brow.

"Thass all very well for you George. I don't know what I'm going to do. It's my belly button. Thass different to everybody elses."

"How different?" asked Charlie.

"Well, that go out, where everyone elses go in. I wouldn't have thought anything about it, but you two were laughing about putting the salt in your belly buttons when we had chips on Friday night. That were bath night and later when I was giving myself a good old soaping down below in the tin bath in front of the fire, I had a good look. You couldn't get salt in my belly button."

We all pulled up our shirts and vests and displayed our belly buttons. Sure enough, Bert's sort of humped itself outwards, while ours went inwards. I picked a bit of fluff out of mine.

"Thass a werry serious matter!" declared Bert.

That did seem a rummon. We quickly tucked our shirts and vests in and saw that Bert was red up to his ears.

"You know Aunt Edith had to finish me off when I was born because old Doctor Bishop was so long a coming. His horse Nelly was on her last legs at the time. Anyway Aunt Edith cut the cord and everything."

"Well, you're still alive," we told him, hoping to cheer him up.

"Yes, but it eernt right."

"You can always keep some salt in a bit of paper," Charlie suggested brightly.

"Corse you can."

You'd have thought that would have settled the matter, but Bert wouldn't be satisfied until he'd talked to the new doctor. We knew his surgery was at his house, about six miles away.

"We can make a day of it. Take a picnic," smiled Charlie.

"We'll go straight after breakfast," I suggested.

The long and the short of it was that we walked along the lanes and cut across a field to the doctor's surgery.

His wife looked surprised to see us outside the door. "What's the matter boys?" she asked.

"Bert's come to see the doctor to see if he's been finished off properly. He go out where he should go in so to speak," piped up Charlie.

"Well, it's a very good question," she answered briskly. "I'll tell the doctor what you're here for." She asked Bert to follow her and left us outside.

We played five stones with pebbles for a bit and the time went quickly enough.

Soon a smiling Bert came out. "The doctor says I'm as right as rain, in fact better than rain in some circumstances such as when there's a village fair on."

We were really pleased and made our way home. All next week we kept wondering if Bert's parent's would get a doctor's bill and what we would say, but they never did.

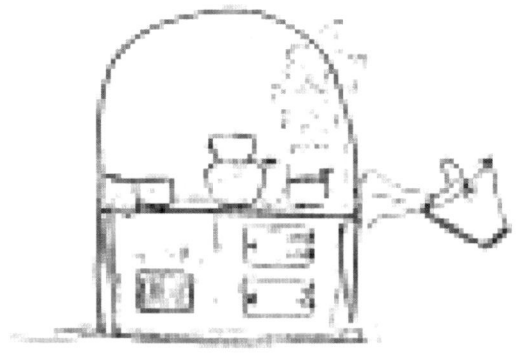

"Some people weren't fussy where they throwed their bucket of water"

Home Cooking

Baking Day was a highlight in the life of us lads. My mouth waters when I start to think of them beef puddings in a cloth and the short cakes! Thass a rummon how sight, touch, smell and flavour all gloriously mingle as you remember a table full of baking and the constant question, "Please mum, can I have some more?"

There was one occasion when mother was poorly. Granny visited and after much whispering they refused to say what was the matter. Only that it was something wrong in that region surrounded by extreme secrecy 'down below'.

Well, one Sunday afternoon father took mother for a little rest upstairs. Charlie and Bert were soon at the door ready to walk to church where Charlie and I helped with the Sunday School classes.

"What's the matter? You look whully upset George," they say.

"Yes, well mother's not up to much and I miss her cooking something rotten. Father's doing the best he can but he can't make a batter pudding to save his life and thass ages since we had a batch of short cakes from the oven."

As I started to talk about food Charlie had an idea.

"Let's face it George we're not much cop with this Sunday School business. I feel a bit of a raspberry trying to lead the little'uns in 'Jesus wants me for a Sunbeam'. One of the little perishers asked me why Jesus didn't want me for a moonbeam, last week and I didn't know what to say. They all giggled and the Sunday School superintendent looked in and demanded why anyone was laughing on a Sunday."

Bert hadn't heard all that as he had been waiting around outside being as how he was a Methodist.

"No, we'll really be useful today," Charlie continued.

"We'll stay here and make some short cakes. Your dad and mum won't be able to thank us enough George."

We soon set to work with gusto. Charlie was a dab hand at pastry and soon had it all rolled out. I spread a thin layer of lard over the pastry and Bert pressed in the currants. Then we folded it over, rolled it out and did the same thing again. In fact all was well at this stage.

We put the roughly cut square shaped short cakes in the greased tins and into the oven which was part of the kitchen range. Then we went out for a walk. Howsomever, what we didn't know was that owing to all the extra worry of mother being poorly, father hadn't cleaned the chimney and the soot had built up.

It didn't seem long afore we saw people rushing along towards us with buckets. "George, your chimney's on fire!" shouted Bert's dad.

Horrified we ran back and saw huge flames shooting out from the chimney and what was worse they were starting to creep along the thatched roof.

Father and mother had been rudely awakened by the neighbours shouting and deciding which bits of furniture should be taken outside. We didn't lock our doors in those days.

I heard someone shouting, "Get the grandfather clock out!" father told us later. He and mother were soon downstairs. Mother was in her dressing gown in the garden looking a bit stunned when we saw her.

All the village had turned up to help out and a chain of buckets was soon organised with father at the lead.

"The Fire Brigade's here!" everyone shouted. "Make way!"

The horses had galloped hard and they were gleaming after all their exertions. The firemen set to work hosing water on the flames and they used grappling irons to pull off the thatch in the middle of the roof to stop the fire spreading.

It would have been really exciting if I hadn't felt that somehow I was responsible for all this and on Sunday, the day of rest too.

We hadn't been able to get near the oven for the crowd of people but we knew the short cakes would be cinders now. What a waste. All in all I felt very worried and upset. Bert looked mournful and even Charlie was serious for once.

"Thass no use you looking so glum, George," father smiled at me. "It could have been worse. The whole house could have burnt down."

I shuddered at the thought of what might have happened.

"The firemen have done a marvellous job and you lads helped out with the best of them. It's good to think people can be so helpful."

Charlie's mother came to have a word with father. "Bring your family over later when everyone's gone and the place is cleared up a bit. I've got some short cakes left over from baking day."

'Short cakes, oh dear', I thought.

Us lads worked really hard to clear up. I still felt mortified to think I had started all this. It wasn't so much the fire as the water which made such a mess. Some folk weren't very fussy where they aimed but of course they had all meant well.

Mother say, "I can't understand how the soot caught on fire with nothing in the oven."

I felt my neck go red. "We thought we'd help out and make some short cakes," I muttered.

"I know you did," broke in father, "and it could have happened if I'd tried a Sunday roast. I miss your mother's cooking too lad. I'm glad you owned up. Do you think you could cope with one of Charlie's mother's short cakes? It will be different to your mother's.   She may make round ones!" Father saw the funny side and started to laugh.

That's one of life's little mysteries that everyone makes a different short cake but no-one makes them like they did in the olden days!

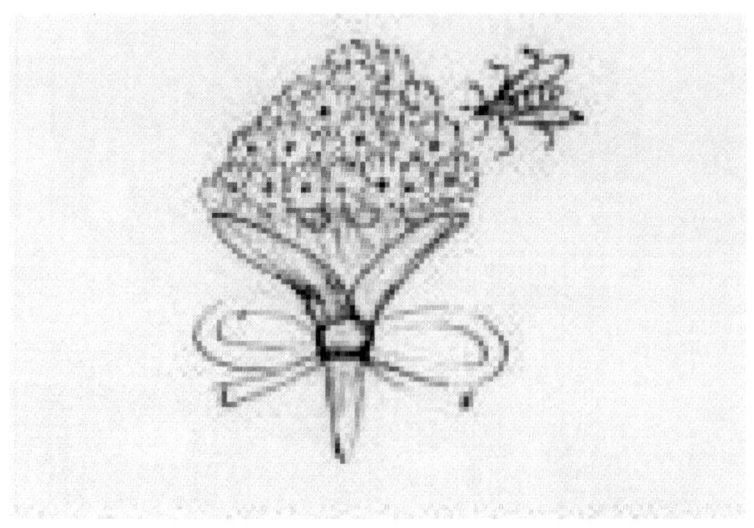

"A wasp started to buzz round the Bride's bouquet."

The Blushing Bride

Charlie and I whully looked forward to choir practice. Us lads liked to see the mawthers and we'd write messages to each other and pass them along the pews. If there was going to be a wedding on Saturday we might get a coin or two to spend and hopefully have some food at the reception.

By rights Bert shouldn't have been to choir practice in the village church seeing as how he was Methodist. His mother had told him to keep out as John Wesley wouldn't like it if he'd known.

"Hold you hard, Bert," argued Charlie. "John Wesley's not around to know and even if he was, he probably had a pal or two to keep him company who weren't Methodists when he travelled about."

"We're just John Wesley's sort - ordinary folk," I told him.

"That's as may be, George," say Bert, "But I darsen't set foot in the choir stalls. There'd be a rare to do."

Charlie had an idea. "Why don't you come and pump the organ? That's a boring old job pumping up and down, up and down. We usually take turns but if you did it, we wouldn't be losing your company."

After a bit of persuasion, Bert joined us one evening. The choirmaster was a bit dubious. "Well, I don't know. I don't suppose it will hurt. We're short of singers now Nobby's voice has broken so you will be helping out. A friend in need is a friend indeed my boy."

Bert was raring to go and he did seem to have a lot of patience and a strong right arm. We were practising for the wedding of Molly Monks, a hulking great mawther, to Sidney Nunn who was a diddy little chap whose mother was a rare one for a mardle. "That Mrs Nunn, she'd talk the hind leg orf a donkey," people used to say.

The couple had chosen to have 'Love Divine', and what with us choir boys grinning and whispering about her changing from a monk to a nun and whether what she'd been up to in the old barn could be called, 'Love Divine', the choirmaster had a rare job to keep our minds on what we were supposed to be a doing of.

The following Saturday, the bells rang out for the three o'clock wedding. We were in the choir stalls in good time in our robes, "looking as if butter wouldn't melt in their mouths," as my mother used to say to Charlie's mother. As usual she probably replied, "Little do they know!" She of course was referring to the congregation looking at us but ironically there was a little that we didn't know.

Unbeknown to Bert, Mrs Nunn had talked to most of the women about her son's wedding, ending up with, "You must come!" Bert's mother had felt she couldn't face Mrs Nunn if she didn't come and have a gawp.

Molly was a sight to behold in a low cut white dress with a lace veil, heaving her way up the aisle on her father's arm to the tune of 'Here Comes the Bride'. Her four bridesmaids dressed in pink came splodging along behind her. When it got to the second line where us choir boys always whispered 'all fat and wide', (very true in this case) Bert saw his mother. Well, he gasped and stopped pumping and the organ wheezed to a standstill. The organist whispered, "Get pumping you lazy lummock!" and Bert set off again.

Bert's mother didn't appear to have seen Bert who kept his head well to the side of the organ. The wedding went off like all the other weddings as far as Charlie and I were concerned. The vicar talked to the couple about the ups and downs of married life and sticking to each other through thick and thin. At the word 'thin' Molly put her bouquet a little further over her bulging stomach and Charlie and I nudged each other.

There were photographs at the end of the service. Molly sat in a chair in the porch with Sidney looking as proud as punch, the best man with them and the bridesmaids either side.

At that moment, a wasp started to buzz round Molly's bouquet. Sidney started to flap it away with his hands. Molly shouted, "Stop it at once Sidney, you're making it angry."

Sidney was that confused he went red in the face.

"Don't you shout at my Sidney like that, young Molly," roared Mrs Nunn. "Sidney was doing his best."

The vicar intervened. "Perhaps someone has a matchbox."

Like a shot, Charlie called out to Bert who was hiding behind a pillar in the church until all was clear, "Have you got a matchbox Bert?"

Of course Bert had got one in his pocket along with various other junk. Out he came, redfaced down the church, with all eyes on him.

He took the itty bitty remains of a gob stopper from his mouth and put it in the match box and after a bit of buzzing about the wasp went and joined it. Bert shut the matchbox up smartish and went well out of church to let it out.

"Be prepared, I always say," smiled the vicar. "Now for the photograph."

Everyone was smiling.

Molly composed her face and Sidney put his arm round her. The best man and bridesmaids got into position again. The photographer got under his cover and the photograph was taken.

Mrs Nunn invited everyone to the reception including the helpful young Bert. "I'm sure you're very proud of your son," Mrs Nunn turned to Bert's mother.

"Oh, er yes."

"You will bring him along . He seems to be making his way across the common. Such a modest boy deserves a treat."

I heard his mother mutter, "He deserves a ding of the lug."

Howsomever she called out, "Charlie and George, please go and tell Bert he's been invited to the reception." Soon we were all enjoying the food. That were a rare good do.

Bert was whully pleased when Mrs Nunn whispered in his ear as he thanked her, "I'll see that you come to the christening too!"

The villagers did a bit of counting when Sidney Junior arrived. Mrs Nunn, a proud grandmother insisted her grandson was very premature.

"Thass a wonder what them doctors and nurses can do to get things moving nowadays," she say.

"Yes," everyone say!

"Charlie's behind looked like a colander covered in small holes"

An Unforgettable Day at Great Yarmouth

Did we laugh? We laughed till we cried! Charlie, Bert and I, having been pals from schooldays through to adulthood, shared many a joke together.

It was the Youth Club trip to Great Yarmouth in old Herbert's charabanc, a real scorcher of a day and we started to sweat a rummon. Well, when we got on the beach our group decided we had got too many clothes on. We would have to disperserate some of them. Some of the more forward ones were even talking about putting on swimsuits.

"Hev you got your swimsuit?" shouted Charlie.

"Yes, but that's getting a bit old."

"Oh, come on. Don't dawdle. Mine came out of the Ark and I'm going in."

Well Charlie put his swimsuit on like lightning. He couldn't wait to get in the sea. His costume was an all in one of navy wool with wide shoulder straps, real Captain Webb ones like the rest of us had in those days, not like the skinny drawers you have nowadays. It didn't look too bad from the front although we could see a small hole in the chest. When he turned round to go down to the sea, - that was a different matter! His behind looked like a colander covered in small holes and one or two larger ones. We started to laugh.

"What's the matter with you two? Why don't you hurry up?"

"It's your swimsuit!" We could hardly tell him for laughing.

"The moths have got in your drawers during the Winter," Bert told him, grinning from ear to ear.

At the word drawers we started to laugh even louder as we saw some other sort of drawers on display. Two of the ladies had tucked up their dresses in their pink lock knit bloomers and were off for a paddle.

"There's nothing wrong with my swimsuit. I'm going in. You two are just jealous that you can't do a belly flop like me."

Off pranced Charlie and we followed, treading carefully over the sharp pebbles until we reached the smooth sand. We couldn't swim but we splashed around and splashed each other.

"Careful. We're getting wet!" laughed the ladies.
When we came out of the water, we struggled to keep our essentials out of sight. The ladies were looking the other way but I noticed their necks were pink.

Charlie couldn't believe his eyes when he had a closer look at the back of his swimsuit.

"Mum will have to get the darning needle out by the looks of it," he chuckled.

"Make sure you ain't in it when she does," we teased him.

It was a great day. We rounded it all off with fish and chips in the paper. How we sloshed on the salt and vinegar.

Going home we made that charabanc ring with our singing, "She'll be coming round the mountain," and sang extra loudly the naughty verse - "She'll have to sleep with grandad when she comes."

A day was all the holiday we got, us lads. All too soon our treat was over for another year. We had good times but none of them topped what we called 'Charlie's bare faced cheek day' at Great Yarmouth!

"It weren't that bare," said Charlie. But he weren't standing where we were.

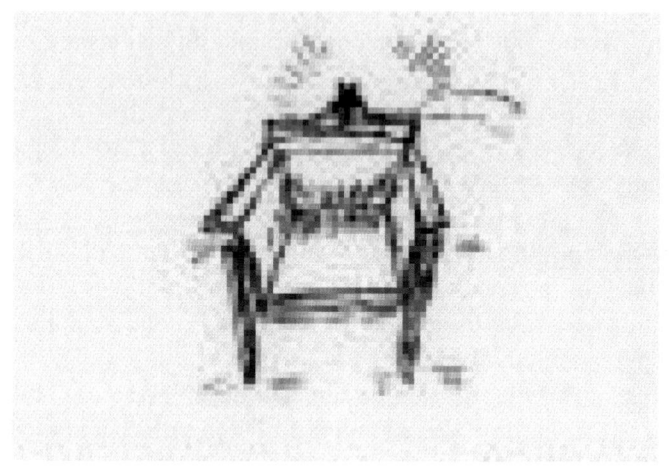

"Ginger bolted right across the fields"

.Down on the Farm

Harvest time was always hot in my boyhood memories. Us lads used to help with taking elevenses and fourses to the men when they stopped for a break.

Bert's father was a farm labourer full time. His employer was one of them whully powerful Methodist farmers. I knew he was very important because Bert told me that when they were in chapel, this farmer would sit at the front with his wife and family. When he thought the preacher had preached long enough, he would get out his big pocket watch on a chain and shake it meaningful like.

"The preacher soon winds up, George," laughed Bert, who was all for short services.

My dad and Charlie's dad used to go as what they called casual farm labourers. My dad was in the building trade. He fell off the top of a ladder when he was doing a bit of carpentering so now he didn't 'aim so high in life', he used to joke. In fact his master put him on to making coffins but he wasn't needed so much in the Summer. Charlie's father was the original Jack of all Trades and instead of being master of none, he was very good at what he set his mind to, albeit with a gammy leg.

The long and the short of it was that one hot sunny morning Charlie, Bert and I headed for the farm with bottles of cold tea, meat pies and hunks of bread and cheese for our dads. The food was in baskets with a cloth on top. Of course we felt a bit stupid carrying baskets. We used to sing loudly to help keep our spirits up,

"To plough and sow and reap and mow,
To be a farmer's boy oy oy!
To be a farmer's boy."

Father said he could hear us coming alright! The men had been working for the best part of sometime when we arrived. Bert's dad waved to us from the bully hole at the top of the stack. He was busy putting the shoofs up on the top. Foreigners who come from outside Norfolk would call them sheaves, so I'll call them sheaves hereafter.

Charlie's dad was in the wagon passing up the sheaves and father was further away putting the binder twine round them with another chap.

It all looked a pleasant enough scene when we arrived. In fact you could have painted one of them police pictures. You know who I mean, him what painted all them bootiful Suffolk places. One of them had got a cart horse. The cart horse hitched to the wagon that Charlie's father was working with was called Ginger.

Well, Bert's father came down the thirty foot ladder easy enough. Charlie's dad got out of the wagon and dad came to see what he had in his basket.

They had just started to tuck in, when Charlie's father say, "Roll us up a cigarette boy."

"Thass your last one," grinned Charlie.

"Here yer are!" handing him a thin, little cigarette he'd rolled for him.

"Now don't drop the packet untidy like will yer."

"No, I'll put it in the basket," say Charlie which he did.

Mind you, first he took the bit of silver paper out of the packet and started to wind it about in his hand. Do you know what? That great cart horse was frightened of that itty bit of silver paper waving about in the sun. That bolted right across the field, out of the gate and into the road. All the harvest workers ran behind and us lads joined them. The faster we ran, the faster Ginger galloped with the wagon clattering along behind. It was downhill to the common.

"Whoa, steady now, steady." Steady wasn't really the word. Ginger was far from steady and the ladder on the back of the wagon to help to hold more sheaves came adrift.

An old lady coming up the hill was scared out of her wits to see the horse and wagon out of control. She jumped into a gateway and sat down, her with rheumatics too. We heard later she broke the eggs she was carrying.

Luck was with us. The gate across the bottom of the lane to stop the animals wandering across the common was closed. So this time it stopped an animal getting on the common and doing much damage.

Ginger saw the gate, slowed down, sweating but unhurt. He calmly let Bert's dad talk to him, stroke him and lead him back to the harvest field.

"I don't know what all the fuss was about," he seemed to say.

Charlie hung his head as we made our way back.

"Do you mean to say George, that was this little bit of paper that caused all the trouble?" he asked.

"Put it away," we warned him. "Less said the better."

Charlie hadn't quite finished. "We'll be back with your fourses," he piped up.

"Don't bother lad, we've had enough excitement for one day. We haven't finished our elevenses yet and we really should be back to work."

Charlie's dad was sometimes quite ungrateful for our efforts. On that occasion we were fortunate. As we went back down the lane, despondent as no-one had said thank you, let alone given us a coin, a horse and cart came along. We rushed to open the gate and even remembered to doff our caps. The gentleman was really pleased and threw us a coin. We all doffed our caps again, it was worth it!

By the way, one reason Charlie's father weren't always that

cheerful was because he had an argument with a pitch fork afore he came to our village. You see he was training to be a member of the Household Cavalry but unfortunately when the horses were being mucked out, he had a pitch fork go into his foot. So ended a brilliant career, so they say, as a decision was made for him to leave.

Perhaps working with a pitchfork brought back memories and that was why he didn't remember to say thank you to Charlie for his elevenses that day on the farm.

"The mouse started to eat his Harvest Supper during the service instead of after it!"

Harvest Home

The harvest festival was one of the highlights of the village year when I was a boy. Mind you, it was not so much the service but the harvest supper which followed which us lads looked forward to.

There was one harvest service which was a little different from the rest. Charlie was keeping mice at the time but he swears to this day that it wasn't his mouse that caused the trouble.

The church was packed with all the village folk. There were fruit and vegetables in all the usual places and some unusual ones too. Charlie and I stood in the choir stalls which had bunches of carrots hanging down so that we looked like a row of donkeys looking over the top. It was the men who made us laugh as we took side long glances behind our hymn books.

"Cor look George, your Uncle Jacob's starched collar is so tight that it's throttling him," whispered Charlie.

It was true. Uncle Jacob, the blacksmith, a hefty man, was sitting looking most uncomfortable, red in the face, one hand on his collar and the other mopping his brow with a huge red and white spotted handkerchief. He was in the well worn brown suit which he kept for high days and holidays. Beside him sat his skinny wife, Aunt Mildred who took in dressmaking and had made the neat brown suit she was wearing and also the hat in matching material. We both looked away and smiled as she gave him a sharp nudge to stand up for "We plough the fields and scatter."

Young Bert had found something to amuse him and he gave us a wink. Although he was Methodist he had been allowed for the best part of sometime now to help out with pumping the organ. We soon saw what he had his eye on. A little mouse had put its head out and was trying to nibble a grain of corn. Bert was grinning. That was alright for him, he couldn't be seen. The vicar always told the choir not to jiffle about. Choir boys should be heard and not seen. However, when the mouse ran past the choir stalls and up to the harvest loaf balanced against the altar, next to a sheaf of corn, the vicar rightly looked dismayed and then stopped and adjusted his face before turning back and smiling at the congregation if you get my meaning.

As the mouse started to eat his harvest supper during the service instead of after it, Charlie sprang to the rescue. "The winds and rains obey him," sang the congregation and the choir, but that mouse would not obey the missing Charlie when he tried to catch it. Everyone was laughing and singing at the same time. The mouse by now, frightened out of its wits, looked for a hiding place up the vicar's robes. You should have seen our clergyman dancing and twitching about as the mouse moved around. Well, what do mice do? It was there that our brave friend Charlie managed to get it as it came out of the sleeve and very reverently to my mind took it out of the side door and gave it its freedom. Then he quietly returned to his place at the end of the hymn. The door seemed to clang even louder than usual behind him but Bert and I put that down to his trying too hard.

These were our opinions but the congregation always talked about that harvest service when Charlie brought his mouse into the choir stalls, the chase which took place at the top of the church and the vicar's contortions when he had the mouse up his robes.

As usual when Charlie rushed to help out he was not thanked. In fact we had to plead with the vicar and even his parents that he should be allowed to join in the harvest supper.

Charlie's mother said, "Charlie boy, if you'd laid low and hadn't been the one to catch the mouse no-one would have remembered that you had any mice at home." They were breeding so well that she couldn't be absolutely sure that it wasn't one of his but she gave him the benefit of the doubt, especially as she had seen him take it out of the church to set it free.

A little bit later the blushing Charlie had an urgent need to collect something from home, so Bert and I ran across the common with him, after he had quickly scooped up a little cardboard box by one of the gravestones. Once home he explained that he hadn't let the mouse out because the vicar kept a cat, so he had decided to let it join his own mice. You don't see kindness like that every day.

"Charlie put his hand up to take his cap off and found he'd bought a feather bed!"

Feathers Galore.

We hadn't had an auction in our part of Norfolk for the best part of some time. Us lads liked to go along and have a gawp, so when Charlie told us that old lady Bunting Smith was moving, we were only too pleased to join him and his family to see what was for sale.

Charlie said that his mother had set her heart on a wash stand set and the neighbours reckon that there was one that had never been used which would more than likely be going for a song.

To cut a long story short, we set off in high spirits on a bright clear morning to walk along the country lanes to the other side of the village.

Of course we weren't the only ones a going and by the time we reached 'Last Retreat', a gloomy looking place with smoke pouring out of the huge chimneys there was a good crowd.

We weren't very interested in the furniture but young Bert and I grinned when we saw the wash stand set.

Bert say, "The jug and bowl are alright, but who'd want to use chamber pots with great pink roses on?"

The bidding wasn't that high and the wash stand set was knocked down to Charlie's father by the scrawny sharp eyed auctioneer, for a very modest sum.

"That's cause there's a chip out of the water jug," pointed out Charlie's mother. "But you always have to have one side to the wall."

Well, Bert and myself started a bit of an argumentation between ourselves as to how bad the weather would have to be before we'd use a duzzy chamber pot when there was a bit of what you might call a dilemma.

Charlie's father had noticed that young Charlie had still got his cap on.

"Take you that cap off, Charlie boy," he say. Well, do you know what? Charlie put his hand up to take his cap off and the auctioneer see him and took it to be a bid to buy the feather bed.

"Oh Charlie," whispered his mother, "What have you been and gone and done?"

His father replied, "Don't put yourself out mother, we can do something about it."

"We'll have to put our thinking caps on," piped up Charlie.

"That's enough about caps, young Charlie. It was you who got us into this mess. I've a good mind to make you carry the feather bed back yourself. That'll larn you!"

Howsomever, the carrier dropped both the wash stand set and the feather bed at Charlie's home.

Later Charlie came round really mortified. "Mother's whully upset. She's going to make the feather bed into pillows."

"Jolly good idea," grinned Bert and I.

Then I made a mistake. "Tell you what Charlie, what about if us lads helped your mother to put the feathers into the ticking for the pillows?"

Charlie was stunned at my brainwave. "Thass a very good idea, George. I'll wait till mother has got started, then when she stops to get on with her housework, I'll let you know and we'll be in there like lightning."

Well, a day or two later Charlie say, "Mother's making a start in the copper house tomorrow morning. She's put every thing ready so we could start after tea and give her a surprise."

No sooner said than done, come seven o'clock we were in the copper house. Charlie was as pleased as punch. He got out his pen knife and ripped a hole along one side of the feather bed. Well, you'd never believe it. Them feathers and little titty bits of down went everywhere. I tell you no lie, we were absolutely covered with them from head to foot. We tried to get them back in the ticking but that were hopeless. We needed something to keep the gap closed.

In the end, Charlie rushed indoors to get his mother. He was shaking, he was so upset. That was nothing compared to his mother. Well, she didn't know whether to laugh or to cry.

"Oh, Charlie, you'll be the death of me," she moaned as she came rushing out.

"Get you home, Bert and George, and get yourselves cleaned up."

She didn't even remember to thank us, she was that upset. We rushed down my garden behind the privy and we each helped each other to get the worst of the feathers and down off. They were even up my nose.

Mother guessed what had happened. She hurried round to Charlie's to see if she could lend a hand. Bert's mother wasn't long a following.

Later there were some rare remarks about interfering when you don't know the job.

Mother explained, "You should have made a very tiny hole in one corner of the feather bed and very gently let the feathers into the pillow, taking great care to keep the hole covered at all times."

I muttered, "If you never try, you never learn!"

Her reply was that "Sometimes you can be a bit too trying."

"Old Herbert, last year's Dumpling King."

Dumpling Day

Dumpling Day was a very important day in the social life of our part of Norfolk. No doubt you've heard of it. Dew you have or dew you hearnt, I'm going to tell you about the werry special goings on in our village.

We always had a big dumpling party in the village hall on October 21st which had connections with Nelson our great Norfolk hero.

The women did the cooking and the men put out the trestle tables and generally made themselves useful and us lads had to lend a hand. Just thinking of all them rows of big fluffy dumplings in thick brown gravy really makes my mouth water. Even the year when Bert over peppered the gravy.

We had Norfolk cider or home made lemonade to drink. Charlie and I used to enjoy a good drop of cider but Bert and his family had to stick to lemonade as they were Methodists. There was a rare lot of talking and joking and general merrymaking.

It was traditional to arrive about 6pm looking as much like a dumpling as possible which wasn't very difficult in certain cases. Everyone put on layers of clothes depending on how slim they were to start with. There were those who didn't need more than one jumper. They're the ones who went around saying how much they'd padded themselves out.

Some of the men put socks or small cushions in the front of their trousers but that didn't really look right biologically speaking and they took them out later when they got too uncomfortable. The main thing was to wear something off white, dumpling coloured on top.

After the tables were cleared away, we had some dancing. Of course we always had the Dumpling Dance. Charlie used to rush out to get a partner. Bert would hang back. We walked it through first with old Herbert at the piano and Archie calling out the instructions. This is how it went. You may want to tell them furreners who celebrate Dumpling Day around the New Year.

It was a big circle dance. The man had his partner on his right.

'Hey Diddle Dumpling, my son John',

Everybody took four steps into the middle. Charlie would rush in nearly pulling the mawthers arms out.

'He went to his bed with his stockings on'.

We took four steps back.

'One shoe off and the other shoe on',

Three steps to the left, kick, and three steps back to the right, kick. I kicked my shoe off one year and felt a fule.

'Hey Diddle Dumpling, my son John'.

We faced our partners. The man took his partner by the right arm and passed her by his right side. The man now had his partner on his left and got in position for a new diddle diddle. The piano was played faster and faster until everyone ended up in a dumpling dollop on the floor. If someone called you a dollop, it was a rare form of endearment.

By way of getting our breath back, we had quiet games that those who had celebrated their 21st birthday more times than they cared to remember could join in.

People sat on chairs in a circle and passed round a homemade dumpling coloured felt ball for 'Pass the Dumpling'. If you'd got the dumpling when the music stopped playing you were out. This could be great fun towards the end when there were only a few left. They had their chairs quite far apart and threw the dumpling to each other. The winner was the last one left.

On this particular evening I was last man in. This meant I was Dumpling King and had to be crowned by the Dumpling King, or Queen if it was a mawther, from the previous year.

Well, old Herbert had been King so he took the red cardboard crown off the top of the piano. It had dumpling balls made of cotton wool on the points. He say, "Bend you down a bit George boy," and put it on my head.

"Well done. You are now Dumpling King George," he announced. Everybody grinned and clapped. "The Dumpling King will bring in the story teller," was his next announcement.

Charlie shouted out, "He's in the old two seater!" Howsomever he soon came out very red in the face.

To end the evening it was traditional to turn the lights out and sit round a story teller in the candlelight. He started by telling Norfolk stories like the Babes in Wayland Wood or the Pedlar of Swaffham. Later when the parents had taken the children home to bed, the atmosphere changed as he set the scene for chilling ghost and mystery stories.

After an evening drinking cider, it was hard to tell what was true and what weren't. At midnight when the party ended the women of course were only too pleased to be escorted home, looking over their shoulders all the way. Yes, they were very grateful to the men on Dumpling Day.

Some folk talked about having a Baby Dumpling day round about July but I only heard about that later. Of course, as Dumpling King that year, I stayed to the end but I can assure you I went home with my family, mother saw to that!

Dad on the 'bucket and chuck it'.

Privy Talk

We had an outside privy when I was a lad. My mother and the other ladies used to call it 'The little room at the bottom of the garden'. Father would talk about going down to 'the bucket and chuck-it' in the same way as he would talk about going to the pub. He had much the same smile on his face when he returned.

"I like to sit and contemplate," he would say. Woe betide any of us who disturbed his 'one pleasure in life' as he called it, sitting reading the newspaper squares that we helped mother cut up. People didn't use loo rolls in those days.

Us lads used to call it 'the thunder box' which sounded much more manly. You needed to have courage to get up at dead of night and make your way down the garden with a candle in a jam jar. My candle always blew out. Some nights the wind seemed to reach gale force proportions and though I couldn't see where it came from I knew exactly where it was going as it forced its way under the gap at the bottom of the door.

Looking back, whoever built our privy just hadn't thought it out. Thump, the sound of an apple falling on the roof was magnified enormously by the stillness of the night.

The path up to the privy went straight for a little way past the clothes line with the linen prop sticking out. Then it veered to the left with nettles brushing against your legs. This was just enough to make life difficult when you couldn't see where you were going. The gap at the bottom of the plain brown camouflaged kazi door was just enough for someone when it was light enough to see your shoes to know who was in there.

"Hurry up father," we would say, noting his wellies. Apart from that his pipe would have given the game away.

"I should get extra time," he would complain. "I'm the one who has to empty it. You wouldn't get such good vegetables if I didn't spread it out carefully with straw and dig it in."

Then there was his speciality of how when he dug up the roots of all the new spuds he emptied the bucket straight in. I always tried not to say anything about father being longwinded if I was waiting my turn for the privy on a Sunday morning as I enjoyed my Sunday roast and three veg and I really didn't want to talk or think about emptying privies while I was eating my lunch.

Animal manure played its part too. Mother's rhubarb crumbles were spoilt when he told us how ours happened to be the earliest and the best rhubarb in the village with the aid of a bit of horse manure.

One winter night as I crept down to the privy I heard movement inside. I rattled the door and there was a scuffling.

"Is that you dad?" I called. There was more scuffling but no one answered. Then as I waited something black and furry ran over my foot. I hollered and rushed back towards the house.

Father threw open the window, "What are you making all that noise for George boy?" he shouted. "You'll wake all the neighbours!"

"A great furry creature ran over my foot," I hissed up to the window. "And my candle's blown out."

"I expect it were a rat," explained father.

"It could have given me a nasty bite," I grumbled.

"Well that's miles away now."

Then I had to make a decision whether to go back to the privy to do what I had set out to do or go back to bed and hold tight. The cold weather decided for me and back down the garden I went. All was quiet and I felt a bit foolish for making a fuss and waking up father especially when at breakfast time he brought up the fact that he had been wakened from his slumbers. He also mentioned the large furry animal that had made for my foot and all the hollerin which followed.

"I thought at least you'd seen a big woolly bear," he laughed. "One that hid behind the privy door ready to grab lonely travellers after their long dangerous journey in the night. Did you think it was a big black bear that stood on its back legs and blew your candle out?"

I felt a rare fule I can tell you. Howsomever, he who laughs last laughs longest they say.

It was early Summer when father got his comeuppance. The weather had been warm and dry and mother had warned us, "Look careful like afore you sit down in the little room to see whass buzzing about in the bucket."

Father joined in laughing. "Your behind would look enormous George coming down on them bees and wopses."

Mother pursed up her lips, a sign that enough had been said.

Well do you know what? That very same morning, father sat on a bee that was sniffing round the edge of the privy seat. There was a roar and father shot back into the house, trousers at halfmast, pushing me out of the way shouting for mother.

Mother had the dubious pleasure of removing the bee sting in the front room. Then she asked me to fetch the wash day blue bag to ease his discomfiture. Of course I had to pass the bluebag through the door when she opened it an inch, no peeping allowed.

Mother of course never referred to the incident. It was one of those family matters that were very private. That is, until one day father happened to mention how I'd yelled when the rat had run over my toe.

"That was at night and bees are smaller than rats," she smiled. "I think you should keep quiet. It's a case of the pot calling the kettle black and what with the newsprint on your seat, you were black alright!"

"That goose had a very saucy streak."

The Hissing Christmas Dinner

When Aunt Fanny said that father had a rare good eye, mother was very upset.

"He certainly hasn't got an eye for the ladies."

"No, I don't mean that. I mean a straight eye for a ball," laughed her sister. "Though he must have had a bit of an eye for the ladies dew he wouldn't have married you!"

Come that as it may, both mother and father were whully pleased when father won the billiards competition at the village hall. The prize was a Christmas goose. My job was to fetch it from the squire. Mother was very anxious I should please.

"Now George be sure to thank him for his special kindness in giving such a generous prize."

"Don't forget to doff your cap," added father.

"I don't always wear one," I muttered, not liking all this fuss.

"We don't want any argumentation young George. You'll have to wear one so you can doff it to show you know he's a bit of a toff," replied father.

Charlie and Bert were waiting to go and fetch the goose with me. Both my friends seemed as pleased as punch that father had won it. I pulled down my cloth cap with a shrug hoping the squire would be out. It seemed to me to be totally unfair that I had to touch my cap to him. Why not touch my cap to the knife and scissor grinder? "People are all the same underneath!" I announced to the others.

By the time us lads had had a bit of further discussion on that interesting topic we had arrived at the manor at the top of the hill.

My wish was granted. "Squire's out boys," smiled the trim little maid in her black dress and white pinny.

"George's dad won the squire's goose," piped up Charlie.

"James will help you George, you can see him through the gate over there in the orchard."

Us lads had all taken our caps off at the door so that was alright. We had them in our hands as we walked past the vegetable garden to the orchard.

James stood rubbing his beard as he saw us coming. He looked down at us, hands on his hips and talked in a stuck up sort of voice.

"You're the young man who has come to collect the goose, I believe. I take it these are your men at arms. You're going to need them," and he laughed in a sneering sort of way. "There's your goose."

At the bottom of the orchard, I could see a large white goose very much alive, pecking at something on the ground.

Determined to be bold, I said "Thank you sir," and started to walk towards it. Charlie joined me but Bert sensibly held back. I don't know how I thought I was going to catch it. Without warning the goose came sort of rushing over the ground towards me, wings flapping, sticking out its long neck and hissing. Charlie had run back as it turned. I was soon running behind him, yelling my head off, the goose close on my heels.

James roared with laughter as if it was an enormous joke and then shut the orchard gate with the goose hissing and trying to stick its neck through the bars.

"Well you've had your goose!" he laughed. "I've got important work to do for the squire indoors now. I'll tell him you came but didn't wait to take the goose home." Still smirking he strode off.

We stood in a huddle. Bert looked worried out of his life. "I should have come in with you. That old goose wouldn't have gone for the three of us." As we watched, his face changed. Bert had had one of his inspirationals. "Thass it. We'll all three go after it fully armed."

Charlie piped up, "I'll take my coat off to throw over it. That will slow it down." He pulled his coat off as he spoke. I had a sack I'd brought with me and Bert had found an old stick.

We went back and that old goose led us a merry dance round and round the orchard.

It cackled and hissed and flapped its wings and we dashed after it in hot pursuit. It was the best part of some time before we had it cornered and Charlie hulled his coat over it. I grabbed its neck to stop it pecking and with Bert holding the sack open we managed to shove it in and restrain it. I produced a bit of binder twine from my handkerchief pocket and trussed it up so it wouldn't move. There it was with its beady eyes peeking out of the top of the sack.

Thass likely James had watched all our shinanikins through a window. He gave us a wry grin as we passed with Charlie at the rear holding my cap which I'd left behind. Soon we made our way home with a fairly subdued parcel under my arm, cap askew where Charlie had planted it.

Mother hurried out of the door to greet us.

"George's got your hissing Christmas dinner!" laughed Charlie.

"Well I never!" smiled mother. "Bring it in lads. Fancy squire giving it to you live. Let's have a look. It looks quiet enough."

Thass where she was wrong! Quick as lightning that old goose was out. I'll leave the rest to your imagination but when father came in the goose was on the skullery table with Charlie dishing out orders how to catch it again.

On this particular evening I was last man in. This meant I was Dumpling King and had to be crowned by the Dumpling King, or Queen if it was a mawther, from the previous year.

Well, old Herbert had been King so he took the red cardboard crown off the top of the piano. It had dumpling balls made of cotton wool on the points. He say, "Bend you down a bit George boy," and put it on my head.

"Well done. You are now Dumpling King George," he announced. Everybody grinned and clapped. "The Dumpling King will bring in the story teller," was his next announcement.

Charlie shouted out, "He's in the old two seater!" Howsomever he soon came out very red in the face.

To end the evening it was traditional to turn the lights out and sit round a story teller in the candlelight. He started by telling Norfolk stories like the Babes in Wayland Wood or the Pedlar of Swaffham. Later when the parents had taken the children home to bed, the atmosphere changed as he set the scene for chilling ghost and mystery stories.

After an evening drinking cider, it was hard to tell what was true and what weren't. At midnight when the party ended the women of course were only too pleased to be escorted home, looking over their shoulders all the way. Yes, they were very grateful to the men on Dumpling Day.

Some folk talked about having a Baby Dumpling day round about July but I only heard about that later. Of course, as Dumpling King that year, I stayed to the end but I can assure you I went home with my family, mother saw to that!

Appendix 'A' – Recipes

'That's one of life's little mysteries that everyone makes a different shortcake, but no-one makes them like they did in the olden days.'

1. Short Cakes

Ingredients :-
- 10 oz self raising flour
- 5 oz fat (butter, marg or lard)
- 4 oz currants
- 4 oz sugar
- milk for mixing
- egg for glazing

Method :-
- Make pastry in usual way.
- Roll out to about ¼ inch thickness.
- Sprinkle with currants and sugar.
- Fold over twice and roll out again to about 1 inch in thickness.
- Make criss cross markings with knife on top.
- Cut into shapes, square, oblong or round.
- Brush over with beaten egg.
- Place on baking tray and bake in oven at about 375F, 180C for about 30 minutes.
- Sprinkle with caster sugar.

2. Boiled Beef Pudding in Cloth

A family boiled beef pudding party was the inspiration for 'Dumpling Day'

For the pastry :-
    1 lb plain flour
    5-6 oz suet
    pinch salt
    milk or water to mix for a fairly soft dough

For the filling :-
    1½ lb beef chopped into small cubes
    1 small onion
    1 tablesp gravy powder
    4 tablesp cold water
    seasoning

Method :-
    Lay dough on lightly floured pudding cloth and roll out to about ½ inch thickness.
    Arrange beef and onion in centre, and sprinkle over gravy powder and water. Season.
    Moisten edges of pastry, fold over bringing sides to top. Pinch together to seal well.
    Fold up edges of cloth and tie securely.
    Place in pan of boiling water and simmer for 4 to 5 hours.

3. Dumplings

'Dumpling Day was a very important day in the social life of our part of Norfolk.'

Ingredients :-
- 4 oz plain flour
- 2 oz suet
- pinch salt
- water to mix

Method :-
Prepare by sifting flour and salt together. Mix in suet and make into a stiff dough with water. Form into small balls and boil in pan of water for about ½ hour.

Recipes given to me by my cousin, Mrs Thora Lindenmayer who held the Beef Pudding Party.

Appendix B

Stories in Norfolk Dialect to read aloud

An Unforgettable Day at Great Yarmouth

Did we larf? We larfed till we blarred. It were like this here. Charlie, Bert and me hevin bin pals from school days rite through till we were grown up, shared menny a larf and joke tergether.

That wus the Yuthe Club outen ter Greart Yarmuth in oul Harbut's charabang, a real scorcher of a day an' we started ter sweat a rummin. Well, when we ha' got on the beach our group decided we hed got too menny clothes on. We'd heter dispersereart sum on 'em. Some o' the forrader ones were even torken about putten on swimsuits.

"Hev yew got yar swimsuit?" hollered Charlie.

"Yeh, but thass a'gettin a bit old." I say.

"Oh, cum yew on. Don't dawdle. Mine cum outa the Ark and I'm a'gorn in."

Well bor, Charlie put his swimsuit on loike lightnin'. He coont weart ter get in the sea. His cozzie wus an all in one mearde outa heavy wool wi' greart thick shoulda straps, rearl Captin Webb ones like wot the rest on us hed in them days, not like them there skinny drors yew hev nowadays. That dint look tew bad from the front although we could see a little bitty hool in the chest. When he ha' tarned round ter go down ter the sea, that wus a whully different kettle o'fish! His backside looked like a culander orl covered in little holes, an' one or tew bigga ones. We started ter larf.

"Was up wi' yew tew? Why don't yew get a move on?"

"Thass yar swimsuit!" We could hardly tell him fer larfin. "The moths ha got inter yar drors durin the Winta," Bert say, a'grinnen from ear ter ear.

At the word drors, we started ter larf whully loud as we cocked a snook at sum other sort'a drors on display. Tew o'them there leardies hed tucked up thar frocks in thar pink lock knit bloomas an' were setten orf fer a paddle.

"There's nuthen wrong wi' my swimsuit. I'm a'gorn in. Yew tew are just jealus that yew carn't dew a belly flop like I dew."

Orf pranced Charlie an' we follered, treaden sorftly over them rare sharp stones till we got to the flat sand. We coont swim but we splashed about tergether an' splashed wun anuther.

"Be yew careful! We're getten a soaken," larfed the leardies.

Wen we cum out'o the warter, we struggled ter keep our essentials out'o sight. The leardies were a'looken the other way but I spotted their necks were whully pink.

Charlie coont believe his eyes wen he hed a good look at the hinder part o' his swimsuit. "Mum'll heter get out the darnen needle by the looks on it," he chuckled.

"Mearke sure yew aernt in it when she does," we teased him.

It wus a greart day. We rounded it orf wi' fish an' chips in the pearper. How we sloshed on the salt and winegar. Gorn hoome we mearde that charabang ring wi' our singen, "She'll be comen round the mounten," and sang extra loud the norty verse, "She'll heter sleep wiv grandad when she cums."

A day wus orl the holiday we got, us lads. All too soon our treat wus over fer another year. We hed good times but none on em beat wot we called 'Charlie's bare fearced cheek day' at Greart Yarmouth!

"It wornt that bare," sed Charlie. But he wornt standen where we were.

Harvest Home

The harvest festival wus wun o' the highlights o' the village year when I wus a boy. Mind yew, it wornt so much the sarvice but the harvest suppa wot cum arter that us lads looked forrard to.

There wus won harvest sarvice that were a mite diffrunt from the rest. Charlie wus a keepin mice at the time but he swear to this day that it wornt his mouse wot caused all the conflopshun.

The church were whully packed wi' a scalder o' willage folk. There wus fruit and veg in all the usual plearces and sum unusual ones too. Charlie and I stood there in the choir stalls what hed great bunches o' carrots hangin down so we looked like a row o' donkeys lookin over the top. It were the fellas wot mearde us larf as we garped from behind our hymn books.

"Cor look George, yore uncle Jearcob's starched colla is so tight that fare to quackle him," whispa'd Charlie.

It wus true as I stand here. Uncle Jearcob, the blacksmith, a hefty great chap, wus sittin looken orl o' a muckwash, red in the fearce, one hand on his colla and the other a moppen of his brow wi' a huge greart red and white spotted handkerchief. He wus in his Sunday best , a well worn, brown suit wot he kept for high days and holidays. Longside o' him sat his squinny wife, Arnt Mildred, who took in dress mearkin and had mearde the titty neat brown suit she wus a'wearin and also har hat in the searme material. Us lads looked away and smiled as she give him a poke in the ribs to stand up for "We plough the fields and scatter."

The boy Bert hed found suffin to tickle him and he gi' us a wink. Bert wus one o' them there Metherdists. He'd bin allowed fer the best part o' some time now to give a hand with pumpen that ole organ. We soon saw wot he hed his eye on. A little mouse fare to ha put its head out and were a' tryen to nibble a grain o' corn. Bert wus a grinnen. That wus alrght fer him, he coont be seen. The wicar allus told the choir not to jiffle about. Choir boys should be heard and not seen. Howsomever, when the mouse ran parst the choir stalls and up the harvest loaf wot wot wus balanced agin the altar, next to a sheaf o' corn, the wicar hed every right to look dismearde and the he fare to stop and put his fearce strearte afore he tahned backards and smiled at them there folk in the congregeartion if yew git my drift.

As the mouse started eaten his harvest suppa duren the sarvice, instead of arter it, Charlie sprang to the rescue. "The winds and waves obey him," roared out the congregation and the choir, but that there mouse woont obey Charlie when he hed a go at catchin on it. Everyone fare to larf and sing at the same time. The mouse wus in a right puckaterry looken fer a hidin' plearce up the wicar's robes. Yew shudda seen our wicar darncen and twitchen about as the mouse moved around. Well bor, what dew mice dew? It wus then that our brave friend Charlie managed to git it as it came out o' the sleeve and right reverently to my mind took it out o' the side door and give it its freedom. Then he came back to his plearce at the end of the hymn. The door fare to clang even louder than usual but Bert and I thort as how he wus a tryin too hard.

These were our thoughts on the matta, but the congregation allus torked about the harvest sarvice when Charlie brort his mouse into the choir stalls, the squit wot went on at the top o' that there church and the wicar's contortions when he hed the mouse up his robes.

As usual when Charlie rushed to lend a hand he wornt thanked. In fact he hed to plead wi' the wicar and even his own parents that he shud come and join in the harvest suppa.

Charlie's mother she say, "Charlie boy if you'd a laid low

and hent bin the one to catch that there mouse no-one would ha' remembered that yew hed any mice round ours."

They were a' breedin so well that she coont be really sure that it wornt one of his but she give him the benefit o' the doubt, more so as she'd sin him tearke it out o' the church to fare to set it free.

A little bit learter, the red fearced Charlie hed an argent need to git suffin from home. So Bert and I ran acrorss the common wi' him, arter he hed quickly scooped up a little cardboard box wot wus by one o' them there grearve stones.

Once home he fare to explain that he hent let the mouse go corse the wicar kept a cat, so he'd mearde up his mind to let it join his own mice. Yew don't see kindness like that every day.

Privy Talk

We had an outside privy when I was a lad. My mother and the other leardies used to call it 'the little room at the bottom of the garden'. Father woud talk about gorn down to the bucket and chuck it in the searme way as he would tork about gorn to the pub. He had much the searme smile on his fearce when he cum back.

"I loike to sit and contemplearte," he would say. Woe betide any on us who distarbed his 'one pleasure in life' as he called it, sittin readen the newspearper squares what we helped mother cut up. People didn't fare to use loo pearper in those dearze.

Us lads used to call it 'the thunder box' which sounded much more manly. Yew needed to hev a rare lot o' courage to get up at dead o' night and mearke your way down the garden with a candle propped up in a jam jar. My candle allus blew out. Some nights the wind whully roared and seemed to reach giant proporshuns and though I couldn't see where that cum from, my hart I knew exactly where it was a' gorn as it forced its way under the gap at the bottom o' the door.

Looken back, whoever built our privy just hadn't thought it out. Thump, the sound of an apple fallin on the roof wus magnified enormously in the pitch black quiet o' the night. The parth up t' the privy went strearte for a little way parst the clothes line wot hed the linen prop a' poken out. Then it sorta veered t' the left wi nettles wot brushed agearnt yor legs. This was jest enough to mearke loife differcult when yew couldn't see where yew were a gorn. The gap at the bottom o' the plearn black camuflaged kazi door were just enough for someone when that got light enough to see yar shoes to know who wus in there.

"Hurry yew up father," we would say, a' seein his wellies. Anyway his pipe would hev given the gearme away.

"I ought to get extra time," he would complearn. I'm the one who has to cum and empty it. Yew wouldn't get such rare good wegetables if I didn't spread it out carefully wi straw and dig it in."

Then there his speshalty o' how when he'd dug up the roots o'all the new spuds he emptied the bucket streart in. I allus tried not to say about father bein long winded if I were a waiten my tarn for the privy of a Sunday morning as I enjoyed my Sunday roast and three weg and I really didn't want to tork about emptyin o' privies while I was eaten my lunch.

Animal manure pleared its part too. Mother's rhubub crumbles were spoilt wen he told us how ours just happened to be the arliest and best rhubub in the willage wi the aerd of a bit o' hoss manure.

One Winter night as I crepp down the privy I heard suffin a movin wot fare to be inside. I rattled on the door and there wus a rare scufflin.

"Is that yew dad?" I called. There wus a hull lot more scufflin but no one answered. Then as I stood waitin suffin black and furry ran over my foot. I hollered and rushed back towards the house.

Father threw the winda open."Wot are yew maerkin all that hullabaloo for George boy?" he hollered "You"ll wearke all the neighbors!"

A greart furry crittur ran over my foot," I hissed up to the winda. And my candle fare t' a blown out."

"I expect that were a rat," explearned my father.

"It coud ha give me a rare nasty bite," I grumbled.

"Well thass miles away now."

Then I ha t' mearke a decishun whether to go back to that there privy to do wot I hed set out to do or go back to bed and hold tight. The cold old weather decided me and I mearde my way back down the garden. All wus quiet and I felt a bit of of a fule for mearkin a fuss and wearkin up father speshully wen at breakfast time he brought up the fact as how he hed bin wearkened from his slumbers. He also menshunned that there furry animal wot hed made for my foot and all the hollerin wot follered.

"I thought at least yew'd sin a big wooly bear," he larfed. "One that hid behind the privy door all ready to grab lonely travellers arter their long and whully daingerous journey in the night. Did yew think it wus a whoppin great black bear wot stood on its hinda legs and blew yore candle out?"

I felt a duzzy fule I can tell yew. Howsomever, he wot larfs larst larfs longest they say.

It were arly Summer wen father got his comuppance. That were like this here, the weather hed bin warm and dry and mother hed warned us, "Look careful like afore yew sit yerself down in the little room to see whass buzzin about in the bucket."

Father joined in the larfin. "Your behind would look enormous George cummin down on them there beez and wopses."

Mother pursed up har lips, that meant enough hed bin said.

Well dew yew know what? That self searme mornin, father sat on a bee wot wus sniffin round the edge o' the privy seat. There wus a roar and father shot back into the house, trousers at half mast, pushin me out o' the way shoutin for mother.

Mother hed the dubious pleasure o' tearkin out the bee sting in the front room. Then she arsked me to fetch the wash day blue bag to ease his discomfiture. Of course I hed to pass the blue bag through the door when she opened it, no pokin yer snout in.

Mother o'course never said nuthin about the incident. It were one of them there family matters that wus werry private. That is, until one day father happen t' mention as how I'd yelled when the rat hed run over my toe.

"That wus at night and bees are smaller than rats," she smiled. "I think as how you should keep yar mouth shut. Thass a cairse o' the pot callin the kettle black and wot wiv the newsprint on yore hinderparts, yew were black alright."